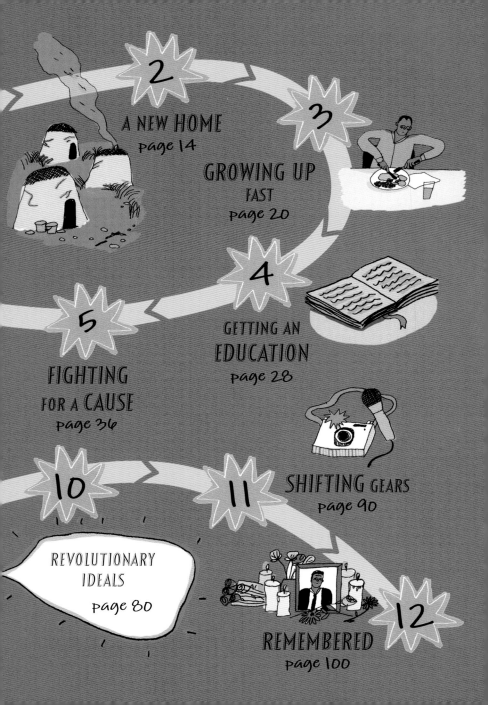

Chapter 1

Troublemaker

**On the day Nelson Mandela was born—
July 18, 1918—his name was not Nelson.
That name would come later.**

At birth, his father gave him the name
Rolihlahla (khol-ee-HLAA-hlaa). Its literal
meaning is "pulling the branch of a tree," but
informally it means "troublemaker." Nobody
claimed that the name was a sign of things
to come—but nobody said it wasn't, either.

Rolihlahla's father, Gadla Henry Mandela,
was a member of the royal house of the Thembu
tribe. His job was advising
people and he was well
respected for his opinions.
Baby Rolihlahla lived with
his mother, Nosekeni Fanny,
in Mvezo (oohm-VEH-zoh).

AFRICA

South
Africa

Mvezo

Mvezo was a village on the Mbashe River. It lay deep in the Transkei, a land of gentle hills and shallow valleys 600 miles (965 km) from the big South African city of Johannesburg.

The Mbashe River winds through the Transkei area.

Their home in Mvezo was called a kraal. A kraal is a small farm, with just a few animals and crops, that could support a single family. Rolihlahla's father saw him at the kraal regularly, but for only a few days at a time. Gadla Henry's responsibilities often took him away from home. He had three other wives and many other children to care for. Rolihlahla was the youngest of his four sons, which did not make him very important.

At the time the native people of South Africa were part of the British Empire. Dutch colonizers had first arrived in South Africa in 1652, and they had not come just to visit. Instead, they had come to settle, and they spent the next 150 years fighting with local tribes until they finally achieved control over the region.

However, their victory was short-lived. In the 1800s, soldiers and pioneers from Great Britain aggressively settled in South Africa. This led to a series of wars that finally ended with a British victory in 1902. Eight years later, South Africa was granted some independence—but it remained in the British Commonwealth, under the firm control of British and Dutch descendants.

---

what are colonizers? People who create a new settlement in a foreign land. Colonizers of South Africa created settlements without caring what the native people thought.

CLASH OF THE COLONIZERS

The Anglo-Boer War was a war of independence fought between the Dutch descendants in South Africa and the British Empire that ruled them. It began in 1899 and ended with a British victory in 1902.

British troops ride into battle during the Anglo-Boer War.

The British and Dutch control over South Africa included control over the land's native people. Where could they live? What education could they receive? Which jobs could they have? These issues were harshly regulated. Certain jobs gave some people power over their fellow black Africans, but no jobs gave black people authority over their white neighbors.

Little Rolihlahla knew none of this, of course. Even so, the outside world soon intruded on his own life. When he was barely a year old, his father got into a heated disagreement with a local white magistrate. The complaint itself was small—something about an ox—but Gadla Henry made an issue of it by defying the magistrate's order that he look into it. Gadla Henry was a member of his tribe's royal family, a descendant of kings. He felt that a mere magistrate should not be able to order him around.

Gadla Henry may have been right in his belief, but he paid dearly for his views.

What is a magistrate?

A government official who administers certain laws in a specific area. The magistrate in Gadla Henry's town was strict.

Black men, even descendants of kings, held power only with the permission of the all-white government. The members of that government did not like seeing their authority challenged. The magistrate dealt harshly with Gadla Henry, taking away much of his land and fortune. This decision sent a clear message to anyone who might share his views.

Among the possessions the magistrate took away was the kraal where Rolihlahla and his mother lived. Under the existing laws, they had no right to argue with this decision.

All they could do was move.

2

A new home

Rolihlahla's family needed a new home, and they didn't have to look far. Gadla Henry still owned some property, including a kraal in Qunu.

It was a nearby village, home to only a few hundred people. It was smaller than Mvezo, but the land was much the same, with grassy fields and hills fed by bubbling streams.

Gadla Henry's kraal in Qunu consisted of three domed mud huts with thatched roofs. One hut was used to sleep in, and the other two were for cooking and storing food. The floors of the huts were made of crushed "ant-heap," which is the hard dirt above an ant colony. Rolihlahla's family used fresh cow poop to keep the floors smooth. There was a hole in the

roofs for cooking smoke to
escape through. The only way in
or out of each hut was a low doorway.

None of the huts had any wooden
furniture. Everyone slept on mats. Outside,
there were fields to grow crops and pens for
the farm animals. The kraal was not fancy,
but it was a comfortable place to live and it
allowed Rolihlahla's family to be self-sufficient.

In the nearby fields, Rolihlahla learned to
use a slingshot. Like many boys his age, he
became skilled enough to shoot birds out of
the sky. Later in life, he
remembered learning "to
gather wild honey and
fruits and edible roots, to
drink warm, sweet milk straight
from the udder of a cow . . . and
to catch fish with twine and
sharpened bits of wire."

what does
"self-sufficient"
mean?

Being able to survive on your own. Because
Rolihlahla's family grew their own food on
the kraal, they were self-sufficient.

Besides fishing and gathering food, Rolihlahla played games, too. The most popular was called *thinti*. Rolihlahla also spent time mastering the art of stick fighting. This was a kind of swordplay that featured thrusts and parries, feints and lunges. All the while the participants danced back and forth as nimbly as they could.

Rolihlahla liked the time he spent exploring the land and playing games with his friends, but his parents knew he had a quick mind, worthy of great achievements. His parents could not read or write, but his mother wanted Rolihlahla to do both, so they decided to send him to school.

PLAYING THINTI

Thinti was a game that featured two sticks that were used as targets about 100 ft (30 m) apart. Two teams of boys would each defend their target while trying to throw sticks at the other team's target. Whoever knocked down the opposing team's target would win.

Until he went to school, Rolihlahla had always worn the traditional clothes of his village: a blanket that wrapped over one shoulder and pinned at the waist. At the Methodist school his mother had picked, however, the students dressed in the Western style, which meant wearing a shirt and pants.

A shirt was found for him quickly enough, but pants were more difficult, so Rolihlahla's father cut off a pair of his own trousers. They were roughly the right length, but much too big around the middle. However, with a rope tightened through the belt loops, they stayed firmly in place. Rolihlahla knew the pants did not really fit properly, but they were his father's pants. He was proud to wear them.

DID YOU KNOW?

English names were thought to be better than African ones, partly because the British colonizers found them easier to say.

One of the first things Rolihlahla's teacher, Miss Mdingane, did with the new students was to give them each an English name. At the time, being called by an English name was considered better than being called by an African one. Since the boys were about to receive a British education, the teachers believed each student should have an English name to match. The British didn't believe African culture was important. They thought British culture was superior.

From the moment Miss Mdingane gave him his English name, Rolihlahla would never be known as such to anyone outside his family again.

What does "superior" mean?

Better than something. The British thought that their culture was superior to African culture.

His new English name was the only one that would be used in school, and it was the name he would be known by from that day on.

Rolihlahla never learned why Miss Mdingane picked the name for him that she did. It was true that his new first name was the same as the last name of famous British naval hero Admiral Lord Nelson—but Rolihlahla didn't know if that was the reason he got it. All he knew for sure was that from that day on, he was known as Nelson.

Growing up fast

For the next two years, Nelson's life in Qunu was comfortable. He went to school, did chores around the kraal, and played with his friends.

One night, though, Nelson's father arrived home at an unexpected time, and the reason for this soon became clear. Gadla Henry was very sick. He had trouble breathing, and could barely move. A few days later, he died.

Naturally, the death of his father was a significant moment in Nelson's life, but its importance went beyond losing a parent. Shortly afterward, Chief Jongintaba Dalindyebo, whom Gadla Henry had long advised, became Nelson's guardian.

what is a guardian?

A person who is responsible for a child. The chief became Nelson's guardian and looked after him as one of his own.

Nelson's mother, Nosekeni Fanny, told her son that he was to be sent away to the king's home, known as the Great Place, in a village called Mqhekezweni (mu-KEH-zuh-when-ee). Nosekeni Fanny knew that by going away, the opportunities that would open up for Nelson would be far beyond what his mother could provide for him. Although she knew she would miss her son, his mother wanted the best for him.

Nelson adjusted quickly to his new life. He missed his mother, but, as he later wrote,

The king's compound in Mqhekezweni

This photograph of Chief Jongintaba Dalindyebo and his wife was taken in 1930, which was around the time Nelson came to live with them.

he found Mqhekezweni to be "a magical kingdom; everything was delightful . . . When I was not in school, I was a plowboy, a wagon guide, a shepherd. I rode horses and shot birds with slingshots and found boys to joust with."

Nelson did well in school and got along well with Jongintaba's son, Justice, and daughter, Nomafu. He ate what they ate and wore what they wore. Jongintaba and his wife treated Nelson fairly and with care. "Jongintaba was stern, but I never doubted his love," Nelson later said. The chief affectionately called Nelson by the name *Tatomkhulu*, meaning "grandpa," because Nelson so often looked very serious.

Not everything was easy, though. At home in Qunu, everyone simply used their

fingers to eat, but in Mqhekezweni forks and knives were the custom. Nelson was not used to them, and he was embarrassed about looking clumsy at meals. There were days when he ate less than he wanted for fear of looking foolish while fumbling with his utensils.

As time passed, the two anchors of Nelson's life became his education and his time in church. Until that point he had always considered the white European colonists as helpers to the black native people. Now, as a teenager studying history, geography, English, and the Bantu language Xhosa (KAW-suh), he began to see a different picture.

Visitors who came to the Great Place, especially a chief named Joyi, expressed the idea that the African people had been far better off on their own before the white men arrived. Nelson's emerging sense of

Christianity was also troubled by the limitations imposed on black people. He believed the church was the ultimate moral guide for how people should behave toward one another—but if this were true, he wondered, how could the church support the oppression of the black people in its community?

At 16 years old, Nelson had reached the age at which the tradition of his tribe expected him to become a man. As a man he would be able to marry, own property, and participate in tribal ceremonies. In order to achieve his new status, Nelson, along with 24 other boys his age, took part in several rituals to mark this important occasion.

Nelson felt an understandable pride and satisfaction at having reached this point in his young life. His mood was sobered, though, by the main speaker of the day, Chief Meligqili

(mel-leek-qwee-lee). Even years later, Nelson was to remember the chief's grim words.

"There sit our sons," said Chief Meligqili, "young, healthy, and handsome, the flower of the Xhosa tribe, the pride of our nation." However, Chief Meligqili was not hopeful about their futures. He declared that all black South Africans were "slaves in our own country." Therefore, the harsh truth was that the hopes and dreams of the boys would never be fulfilled. This was because the boys could not receive "the greatest gift of all, which is freedom and independence."

"We have promised them manhood ... a promise that can **never be** fulfilled."

Chief Meligqili,
as quoted in Nelson's
autobiography, *Long
Walk to Freedom*

Chapter 4

GETTING AN education

Nelson did not live at a time or in a place where he could expect to choose his own future. That decision was in the hands of Chief Jongintaba.

In the chief's eyes, the first thing Nelson needed was a more complete education. One day, if all went well, he expected that Nelson would become an advisor much like Nelson's father had been before.

Nelson was sent to the Clarkebury Boarding Institute, in the town of Ngcobo. The school buildings were Western in style rather than African.

Nelson was introduced to the headmaster, the Reverend Mr. Harris, in his study. The reverend was warm and friendly toward Nelson, and they shook hands. Nelson was to remember later that it "was the first time I had ever shaken hands with a white man."

In his old school, Nelson was respected because the chief was his guardian— but at Clarkebury, nobody knew who Nelson's guardian was. And nobody cared. At Clarkebury, only Nelson's abilities and achievements would set him apart. Nelson knew that gaining respect from his teachers and fellow students would not be easy, because he had not yet excelled inside the classroom or outside on the playing fields.

In the beginning of his time at Clarkebury, if Nelson stood out at all, it was because he looked like he didn't belong. On the first day

of classes he had
to wear boots for the
first time, and his feet clattered so much on
the polished wooden floors that some of his
classmates laughed at him.

Three years later, in 1937, when Nelson
was 19 years old, he moved on to Healdtown.
Healdtown was a Methodist college in the town
of Fort Beaufort, almost 200 miles (325 km) away.

Nelson at 19
years old

At first, Nelson felt that it
was almost like visiting another
planet. Flush toilets were new
to him. So were pajamas and
toothpaste. (Before coming
to Healdtown and learning
what toothpaste was, Nelson
whitened his teeth by rubbing
ash on them.)

The schedule there was rigorous. Breakfast was early, at 6:40 a.m., and it was nothing more than dry bread and hot sugar water. The morning was filled with four hours of classes. Lunch,

Samp was often mixed with beans.

which was at 12:45 p.m., usually featured sour milk and beans, and dried corn kernels, called samp. Classes continued for another four hours, followed by a break for exercise and dinner. An evening of homework ended with lights out at 9:30 p.m.

At Healdtown, Nelson participated in school sports for the first time. He took up cross-country running and boxing, both of which took discipline and helped him fit in with other students. At first he was not especially good at either, but through practice—and by gaining a few more pounds of muscle—he soon improved.

As for his classroom education, Nelson was not just gaining academic knowledge.

DID YOU KNOW?

While attending Fort Hare, Nelson took ballroom dancing classes.

He was also gaining a better understanding of the limitations a black man faced in the white man's world. This growing awareness continued to build as he moved on to the University College of Fort Hare, in the town of Alice, in 1939. There, as at his other schools, he remembered being taught that he should respect the political authorities and be thankful for the educational opportunities given to him by the church and by the government.

As his thinking grew more sophisticated, though, it was difficult for Nelson to make all these ideas fit nicely together. On the one hand, he was being taught to use logic to solve problems and work out situations. On the other hand, he was also being told to accept certain social and political boundaries that were ingrained into society. And these, he was well aware, were not really logical at all.

Being clear about his ideas helped Nelson to develop a new sense of independence. In his second year at Fort Hare he was elected to the Student Representative Council. When the university administration refused to grant the council some of the authority the council believed it should have, Nelson resigned in protest. He had the power to do that—but the university had power, too. The principal chose to send him home early for what he called insubordination.

what is insubordination?

Insubordination means to disobey an order from a higher authority. The headmaster judged that Nelson was insubordinate when he resigned from the school council.

Chief Jongintaba was surprised and displeased to see Nelson come home before his term at Fort Hare was over. He made it clear to Nelson that he, the chief, was in charge of Nelson's life. The boy should simply do as he was told. To make this point even clearer, the chief soon informed Nelson that he had chosen a wife for him to marry.

Now it was Nelson's turn to be surprised. He didn't know if arranging a marriage was the chief's way of reminding him who was the boss in their relationship or whether he genuinely thought this young woman was the perfect partner for Nelson. Either way, he knew better

ARRANGED MARRIAGE

It was common in many societies (and still is in some cultures today) for parents or guardians to arrange the marriages of their children. The reasons behind the matchmaking were often quite practical. Money was a common factor, because the fortunes of two families would be joined together by the union. Or it might be that the two pairs of parents simply liked the idea of their families becoming related through marriage.

than to argue because, as his guardian, the
chief had the traditional right to arrange such
a marriage. Yet that didn't mean Nelson would
meekly accept his decision. Nelson was stubborn,
just as his father had been, but he knew he could
not refuse the arranged marriage and continue to
live under the chief's roof. His only alternative
would be to run away.

And so, in 1941, at the age of 22, he did.

Chapter 5

Fighting FOR A cause

When Nelson decided to run away, there was no question about where he would go. His destination was Johannesburg.

In Johannesburg, the largest city in South Africa, Nelson believed he might be able to improve his social status and achieve his goals. He was also very excited to see a place he had heard so much about. In his mind the city had almost a mythical status.

The city of Johannesburg as it looked in the 1940s

Johannesburg was not simply a larger version of a town. He had been told stories of "buildings so tall you could not see the tops, of crowds of people speaking languages you had never heard of . . ." What should he do once he got to

Johannesburg? Nelson wasn't sure. He hadn't done much planning in advance, so it took him some time to settle in. He worked as a night watchman in a mine and as a real estate agent while he finished his college degree with courses he completed through the mail.

For all the time that he was growing up, Nelson had always imagined himself returning home to Qunu at some point to take up a career. In 1943, he enrolled in law school because it seemed like the logical next step,

"Johannesburg had always been depicted as a city of dreams, a place where one could transform oneself from a poor peasant to a wealthy sophisticate ..."

Nelson Mandela,
Long Walk to Freedom

but he did not really apply himself to his courses. And, in the end, he did not complete the requirements for graduation.

Nelson had only been in Johannesburg a short time when he started to focus more on political activism. He wanted to change things in the government. The central problem facing black people in South Africa was the crushing oppression they met at every turn. Black people were kept down and not allowed the same opportunities or freedoms that were allowed to others. After the British created the Union of South Africa in 1910, new laws were designed and enforced to keep black people from pursuing any number of careers.

FORGIVE AND FORGET

Toward the end of 1941, Nelson's guardian, Chief Jongintaba, visited Johannesburg and met with Nelson, forgiving him for running away. Jongintaba died only a few months later.

It didn't matter how smart they were or how hard they worked. They were trapped in a web of regulations to keep progress out of reach. Nelson clearly saw the widespread injustice in this system, and he was determined to do something about it and help his people.

To make sure his efforts were as effective as possible, he joined the African National Congress (ANC). The ANC was an organization trying to improve the conditions for black South Africans. Its protests, though, were largely very

NEW LAWS

In 1911, the Mines and Works Act was passed. It meant that black South Africans worked in low-paying jobs. The more skilled, higher-paying jobs, such as surveying, were reserved for whites. Two years later, the Natives Land Act severely limited where black people could own land. Even when they were allowed to own it, this land had little value. It was always set deep in the countryside away from the cities. Could black people hope for change to come through the political process? Not really. The Native Representation Act of 1936 meant that only elite (high-class) black people could vote, the majority couldn't, and they could only vote for white candidates.

The ANC had its roots in the South African Native National Congress. Some of its members are shown here in 1914.

polite efforts. Petitions would be circulated and signed by black people. These petitions were then submitted to the white authorities, who would either ignore them or bury them in administrative red tape.

The aim of Nelson and his friends was to transform the ANC from a small group

what does "red tape" mean?

Red tape is lots of unnecessary paperwork demanded by governments or big businesses. The South African authorities used red tape as a way of avoiding dealing with the petitions.

of intellectual activists into a much larger organization. It would have a mass membership of black people from all over the country. Educated or not, these people had never been given the chance to speak up. They had suffered largely in silence. Maybe now their voices would be heard.

As a first step, Nelson and some others created the African National Congress Youth League in 1944. They intended to change things politically, to make life better for black people. They wanted more rights relating to voting and land ownership.

Walter Sisulu

They called for free education for all children regardless of their skin color. Nelson was passionate about these issues, but he still had a personal life. One of his friends in the ANC, Walter Sisulu, had a cousin called

Here's Nelson.

This is Evelyn.

Nelson and Evelyn, as bridesmaid, were guests at Walter Sisulu's wedding.

Evelyn who was a nurse. She and Nelson soon started dating, and a few months later they were married. For now the pieces of Nelson's life had fallen into place. Yet even though those pieces seemed to fit together well, it was not clear how long they would continue to do so.

Chapter 6

Revolutionary thoughts

Nelson had opposed many South African laws because they kept black people from freely improving their lives.

These prohibitions, bad as they were, soon became much worse. In 1948 the new all-white Afrikaner National Party took control of the government. Soon after that, South Africa made into law the policy of apartheid.

Apartheid formally separated black people from white people in many ways. It kept people apart politically, socially, and economically on the basis of their race. Black people would now have to live in separate areas from whites. Marriages between them were banned. Black South Africans were also separated from one another by their tribal backgrounds.

PROTESTS AGAINST APARTHEID

At first, there was little response from other countries to South Africa's new policy of apartheid. However, some people did form groups to protest. Unfortunately, although these protests received some attention, the laws remained in force.

People protesting against racial discrimination in London, England

This was a political strategy, or plan. If tribes were kept apart, they were unlikely to ever come together to threaten the existing authority.

The government did not even pretend that these changes were at all for the benefit or the good of black people. It was cold and

ruthless in its mission to put black people in their place and keep them there. No change, no new regulation, that would achieve this was too outrageous to propose.

Although the white people of South Africa were comfortable with apartheid because of their sense of superiority, there was another

LAND REFORMS

A few years later, in the 1950s, further steps were taken to strengthen white control. Black people were often forcibly removed from the parts of the countryside where they had lived for generations. The land they left behind was then sold to white farmers at artificially low prices. As white people became increasingly wealthier than black people, whites gained even more control of the country.

reason they wanted
these new laws in place.
That reason was fear.
For all of the power they
held over black South
Africans, white people
were still a minority when it
came to actual numbers. This

knowledge made them nervous. To overcome
this fear, they tried to build up as much support
from the legal system as they could get.

As things turned out, the new policies
triggered huge outrage. The black activists
living in South Africa reacted to apartheid
with renewed energy.

In 1949, the ANC pushed hard to become
a much bigger organization. No longer would
its members be content to politely raise their
hands when objecting to government policies.
Previously, the ANC had tried to keep their
protests within legal bounds—an approach that
had clearly not brought them much success.
Their new strategy would call for more action.

TREASON TRIAL

SED

DECE
195

Nelson Mandela and the other activists were gathered up in raids around the country and arrested for their allegedly treasonous activities. Eventually all of the accused were set free.

They would focus on passive resistance. This meant that their protests would not use violence. There were risks in taking even non-violent actions, but Nelson and his colleagues were willing to accept those risks.

In the next few years, Nelson was repeatedly arrested for joining in protests around the country. In 1952, he was one of the leaders of the ANC's Campaign for the Defiance of Unjust Laws. Nelson was committed to protesting against apartheid whatever the price he might personally have to pay. He worked with the ANC and other organizations to write the Freedom Charter, which set out rules for a fairer society. This led, in 1956–1961, to Nelson and 155 activists being unsuccessfully prosecuted for treason.

In 1952, Nelson founded a law firm with Oliver Tambo, a friend from his former school days. Their aim was not to

Oliver Tambo

make money, although some payment would have certainly been welcome since neither of them had independent sources of income. Their main purpose was to provide free or low cost legal representation to black people in need.

All of this activity, however, came at a price for his family. Nelson's fight against injustice for black South Africans consumed him. Nelson remembered later that it was during this period when his wife, Evelyn, told him that their "elder son, Thembi, then five,

had asked her, 'Where does Daddy live?' I had been returning home late at night, long after he had gone to sleep, and departing early in the morning before he woke."

Evelyn harbored resentments of her own. Certainly, she had married Nelson for love, but her dreams differed from his. Evelyn had expected that his life would be a normal one devoted to his family and a regular job. Nelson wrote that she could not live with him being devoted to something apart from herself and her family. The harder Nelson worked, the more their relationship suffered. They managed to stay together for a few more years, but were finally divorced in 1958.

7

Raising the stakes

Nelson had been committed to non-violent protest. His hope was that the government would see the error of its prejudiced ways.

However, there was a problem. This hope was based on the idea that the government would actually *want* to be shown the error of its prejudiced ways. The South African government wasn't actually interested in seeing this at all. They knew their laws were prejudiced against black South Africans. They knew that these laws would oppress, or keep down, black people and keep them serving the needs of white people. The truth was, they liked things that way.

---

what does "prejudice" mean?

Prejudice is having unfair feelings against certain people. The government was prejudiced against black South Africans.

Nelson and his comrades began to feel that non-violent actions were not the answer. In 1960, a peaceful protest ended in the police shooting dead many protesters. It became known as the Sharpeville Massacre. This terrible event helped confirm to Nelson and his fellow activists that more violent steps were now necessary.

The activists knew that using violence would be dangerous, and they were afraid for their own

SHARPEVILLE MASSACRE

On March 21, 1960, a crowd of several thousand protesters went to the local police station at Sharpeville in the Transvaal. Although the crowd was unarmed, police officers opened fire. They continued to shoot even as the crowd fled in fear. Sixty-nine people were killed and more than 400 were wounded, including women and children. Even under the laws of apartheid, the massacre created a crisis for the government.

Black protesters being fired on by police

safety. However, as Nelson later wrote, "The brave man is not he who does not feel afraid, but he who conquers that fear."

It was just a few years earlier that Nelson had met Nomzamo Winnie Madikizela. She was the first black female social worker ever trained in South Africa and an active member of the ANC. As Nelson later wrote, "I cannot say for certain if there is such a thing as love at first sight, but I do know that the moment I first glimpsed Winnie Nomzamo, I knew that I wanted to have her as my wife."

Unlike Nelson's first wife, Evelyn, Winnie was well aware of Nelson's priorities. His law practice was not going well, but he was unwilling to sacrifice any of the time he was devoting to the ANC. He told Winnie that they would very likely have to live on her small salary as a social worker. Winnie understood and was prepared to do this.

Eventually, after years of peaceful protests, and no changes by the government, Nelson

Nelson married Winnie on June 14, 1958. They later had two children together.

saw violent protest as the only way to get the white minority to listen. In 1961, new tactics began, including planting bombs in places like electrical plants or transportation facilities. Nelson did not pretend that these actions were not violent. However, targets were chosen to avoid loss of life as much as possible.

During this time, warrants were issued for Nelson's arrest. His many friends and supporters helped keep him hidden. He also escaped capture by sometimes traveling in disguise. At one point he drove around the country giving speeches while pretending to be a chauffeur.

However, Nelson's luck finally ran out. He was captured in August 1962 and accused of

False travel documents used by Nelson in 1962

various crimes against the state. At his trial he did not really defend himself. (He actually agreed that he was guilty of the charges.) Instead, he concentrated on promoting the ANC cause. His actions were reluctant ones, he insisted. Desperate times, he argued, called for desperate actions.

The court did not agree. Nelson was sentenced to five years in prison. However, the next year he was found to be connected to other illegal activities against the government. The charges were serious. Once more he was accused of sabotage. A second trial took place between October 1963 and June 1964.

Outside the court, a large crowd gathered to protest. Toward the end of the trial, Nelson made an impassioned speech. His words rang out, not only in the courtroom, but also later throughout the country and around the world.

"During my lifetime," he stated, "I have dedicated myself to this struggle of the African people. I have fought against white domination, and I have fought against black domination. I have cherished the ideal of a democratic and free society in which all persons live together in harmony and with equal opportunities. It is an ideal which I

What does "sabotage" mean?

To destroy or damage a plan or property. The revolutionaries sabotaged power plants to stop them from working.

hope to live for and to achieve. But if need be, it is an ideal for which I am prepared to die."

When the verdict was announced, Nelson and the others were found guilty. They were sentenced to life imprisonment. It was a scary moment. If the sentences were carried out, only death would set them free.

8

Life behind bars

Robben Island lies little more than 4 miles (6.5 km) off the lower west coast of South Africa.

The island had long been used as a place for people who were classed as "undesirables"— people who were not wanted. It had once been a colony for people who suffered from the disease of leprosy. Usually, though, Robben Island served as a jail for political prisoners and convicted criminals. And that was its purpose when Nelson was sent there in 1964.

Nelson and six fellow prisoners faced a difficult journey to the island. They were taken away in the middle of the night, under heavy police guard. They soon arrived at a small military airport and boarded

WELCOME

WELKOM

ROBBENEILAND

WE SERVE
WITH PRIDE

ONS DIEN MET TROTS

This is how the entrance to the Robben Island prison looks today. It is no longer used to keep prisoners, and is now a UNESCO World Heritage site that is open to visitors.

an old plane. The prisoners were frightened, some had never flown before.

Upon arriving on the island, Nelson and the other prisoners were met by armed guards. Nelson remembered the chill winter wind blowing through their thin prison uniforms.

Nelson was initially classified as the lowest grade of prisoner—Class D. This meant that he was allowed one visit and one letter every six months. At first Nelson was housed with several other prisoners, but in later years he lived alone in a small, damp concrete cell. When Nelson lay down, he could feel one wall at his feet while the other end grazed the top of his head. The cell had no mattress or bed, only a flat straw mat to sleep on. As for the food, Nelson later recorded his opinion. He recalled that the authorities liked to say that prisoners received a balanced diet. Nelson agreed that it was balanced—a balance between tasteless and being uneatable.

Every morning, Nelson, along with the other prisoners, waited while a load of stones

This was Nelson Mandela's prison cell on Robben Island.

was dumped on the ground outside. Each one was about as big as a volleyball. The prisoners' job was to crush the stones into gravel using a hammer.

Nine months later, Nelson began working at a limestone quarry. There he extracted limestone from layers of rock

DID YOU KNOW?

At first, Nelson was forbidden to wear sunglasses, and the glare from the limestone permanently damaged his eyesight.

with a pick and shovel. The commander in charge assured the prisoners that this kind of heavy labor would last for six months at most. That turned out to be a lie. The prisoners worked at the quarry for much longer than six months—they worked there for 13 years.

Physical hardships were not the only worries. A prisoner's mental health was always vulnerable. No matter how strong-willed the prisoners were, the prison environment was designed to break them. If the men had been isolated, or kept alone, they might not have been able to survive. Fortunately the authorities kept the prisoners together, and being together, they could draw on mutual support.

Even though he was in prison, Nelson continued to work hard to support people.

"We supported each other and gained strength from each other. Whatever we knew, whatever we learned, we shared ..."

From Nelson's autobiography, *Long Walk to Freedom*

65

He offered guidance and leadership to many of his fellow inmates, representing them in grievances with prison authorities. Gradually, his living conditions improved. In the 1970s, he was allowed more visitors and greater freedom to correspond by mail.

Meanwhile, the force of apartheid continued to oppress black South Africans. On June 16,

High-school students in Soweto, South Africa, protesting for a better education in 1976

1976, between 10,000 and 20,000 children marched in protest in the township of Soweto. The crowd was peaceful and unarmed, but the police became alarmed and eventually began shooting at them. Twenty-three people died in that first response. More protests followed, leading to further deaths.

With Nelson and other leaders in prison, and the ANC barred from the country and in exile, other people took the lead. In the late 1960s another group in South Africa, the Black People's Convention, arose to challenge the institution of apartheid. One of its leaders was Steve Biko, who was threatened several times by the authorities. Finally arrested in 1977, he was severely beaten while in custody. He died from this attack. His death inspired people to continue to protest even more strongly against apartheid.

Such incidents brought the problems in South Africa to people's attention all around the world. Boycotts of South African companies were organized. This meant that people withdrew from

STEVE BIKO

Steve Biko was born in 1946. He was a member of the Xhosa people in the Eastern Cape, a province of South Africa. While growing up, Steve planned to study law, but he changed his mind and decided to study medicine at the University of Natal. However, law again became his focus when he struggled against unjust laws in the fight against apartheid.

trading with South Africa. Many
foreign leaders protested against the
prejudicial system that had been in place for
decades. In 1980, the United Nations Security
Council called for Nelson's release. The request
was ignored.

Through it all, Nelson's spirits remained
strong. "I never seriously considered the possibility
that I would not emerge from prison one day," he
wrote later. "I never thought that a life sentence
truly meant life and that I would die behind bars.
Perhaps I was denying this prospect because it was
too unpleasant to contemplate."

9

Freedom

Although some changes to apartheid took place in the 1980s, the government under President P. W. Botha continued to oppress black people.

Botha, known as "The Great Crocodile," had the reputation of being a stubborn man. In a major speech given in 1985, Botha refused to change the apartheid system. He

was not going to be the one to change a policy and way of life that had been in place for so many years. He also refused to release Nelson Mandela from prison, despite requests from many international figures and organizations.

P. W. Botha

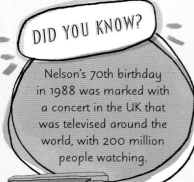

DID YOU KNOW?

Nelson's 70th birthday in 1988 was marked with a concert in the UK that was televised around the world, with 200 million people watching.

Both these decisions sparked strong reactions from the international community. Many countries were now punishing South Africa for its policies by refusing to invest in South African companies. Many international corporations withdrew support as well. The rest of the world was waking up and paying attention to what was happening in South Africa.

Only when a new president, F. W. de Klerk, was elected in 1989, however, did dramatic changes occur. Originally viewed as simply the latest in a long line of apartheid-supporting leaders, de Klerk surprised many onlookers with a more understanding outlook. De Klerk was well aware that the tensions between black and white South Africans were growing. The country might soon erupt into a racial civil war. If that happened, South Africa would be torn apart.

To lessen those tensions, the de Klerk government began allowing anti-apartheid groups to meet. Most importantly, he ordered the release of prisoners who had been convicted for their anti-apartheid activities. Among them was Nelson Mandela.

During the 27 years Nelson had spent in prison, the world had changed in many ways. Important civil rights acts had been passed in the United States. People had landed on the moon. An American president had been forced to resign in disgrace. The Soviet Union had fallen apart. Nations that had belonged to the Soviet Union had again become independent countries.

Also, while in prison, Nelson had suffered two terrible losses. In 1968, his mother died. Just a year later, his eldest son,

In Soweto, an overjoyed boy holds up a newspaper announcing Nelson's release from prison. It made headline news around the world.

Thembi, died in a car accident. Nelson was not allowed to attend the funerals.

Nelson's release in February 1990 ushered in a new era in South African life. He had already met with President de Klerk during the last months of his imprisonment, which helped make sure that de Klerk made good on his promise to dismantle some apartheid restrictions.

One of the first places Nelson visited as a free man was Soweto, the scene of so much violence and unhappiness. There, 120,000 people gathered to hear him speak. Nelson spoke plainly. Injustice, he insisted, was no excuse for unacceptable behavior.

As he emerged from prison, with Winnie by his side, Nelson raised his fist in the traditional ANC salute. The act was met with a great roar from the waiting crowd.

Nelson said that he had heard of criminals pretending to be political activists, preying on innocent people and setting alight vehicles. These criminals had no place in the struggle against apartheid. Violence was not the answer—they must move forward peacefully.

Within a few months Nelson was hard at work within the ANC to build on the changes that President de Klerk had started to set up. He also traveled abroad, meeting with many foreign leaders including Pope John Paul II, Prime Minister Margaret Thatcher of the United Kingdom, and Presidents George H. W. Bush of the United States, Fidel Castro of Cuba, and François Mitterrand of France.

WINNIE MANDELA

When Winnie Madikizela married Nelson, she was viewed as a supportive partner who shared his political views. She appeared loyal during his many years in prison. However, stories reached Nelson that Winnie had been unfaithful. He also heard that she was involved with a violent street gang in her fight against apartheid. In 1995, Nelson dismissed Winnie from her role in his government. Their marriage finally broke down in 1992, and they divorced in 1996.

Several conferences that sought to move things forward were then held within South Africa, but it was unclear at first what the outcome might be. Some South Africans wanted things to continue the way they had before. Others wanted South Africa broken up into more than one country as a way to ensure that black people would have their proper rights.

Several uncertain years passed before the government took on a new shape, one that Nelson and the ANC had worked to create and could support. After more than three centuries

of rule, the white minority was admitting defeat and turning over power to the black majority. In April 1994 new elections were held, and the ANC was swept in to power. Members of the new National Assembly then formally elected Nelson as the country's first black president. It was a truly historic moment, but as Nelson himself said, it did not represent the end of his quest. "We have not taken the final step of our journey," he said, "but the first step on a longer and even more difficult road."

"... to be free is not merely to cast off one's chains, but to live in a way that respects and enhances the freedom of others."

Nelson Mandela, from his autobiography, *Long Walk to Freedom*

10

Revolutionary ideals

The new president of South Africa was 77 years old when he took office. The years Nelson had spent in prison had taken a physical toll.

Nelson had suffered from both tuberculosis and cancer before assuming the presidency. Still, he felt full of new energy at the idea of finally getting rid of apartheid, which had plagued his country for so long. Nelson made a powerful speech when he was sworn in as president: "The time for the healing of

wounds has come. The moment to bridge the chasms that divided us has come. The time to build is upon us. We have, at last, achieved our political emancipation." Nelson meant by this that his people had achieved political freedom.

In a way, Nelson's goal was simple. He wanted to make sure that black people and white people were treated equally. However, achieving this goal would not be simple at all. It was daunting. Nelson did not want to swap one kind of oppression for another, and he didn't want to use force to bluntly and perhaps violently achieve the changes he wanted. He knew certain changes required patience and a delicate touch. "In nation building," he wrote, "you sometimes need a bulldozer, and sometimes a feather duster."

He was also not seeking revenge. The past was filled with outrages and injustices, but he couldn't change the past—although if there were injustices that could be addressed and corrected he certainly wanted to do so. He knew that instituting, or making into law, a new round of punishments would only make people feel bitter on both sides.

What President Mandela hoped and worked for was a peaceful transition, or change, to a new South African reality. He didn't want to punish white people for their past behavior. At the same time he made it clear that this behavior would no longer be tolerated.

Nelson stands to attention as the South African national anthem is played during his presidential inauguration at the Union Building in Pretoria, South Africa, on May 10, 1994.

A supporter waves an ANC flag during Nelson Mandela's presidential inauguration.

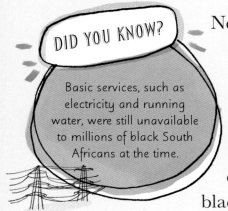

DID YOU KNOW?

Basic services, such as electricity and running water, were still unavailable to millions of black South Africans at the time.

Nelson kept a careful balance between compromise and change. He wanted to ensure that basic human needs of housing and health care were met for everyone, black and white alike. The policies governing land ownership, for example, which had excluded black people for so long, needed a complete overhaul.

All these changes represented a huge upheaval. Nelson, however, was determined to make these changes while keeping racial harmony between the people. One of Nelson's largest concerns, or worries, was South Africa's economic health. The country would be in big trouble if the white population became so afraid or disenchanted that they chose to leave South Africa, taking their skills and resources with them.

what is disenchanted?

Disenchanted means to no longer be in favor of something. Nelson was worried that the white people in South Africa might become disenchanted with the new regime.

"At a time when some of the **most vibrant economies** in the world have been **buffeted by storms,** we have performed relatively well."

Nelson Mandela, from his New Year's message as president, December 31, 1997

In 1996, two years after becoming president, Nelson signed into law a new constitution. It was a historic moment. Freedom of expression would now be available for anyone and everyone regardless of their political leanings. This meant that people were free to speak out about their beliefs. These changes reflected Nelson's idea that a government could not only survive, but actually improve, from listening to criticism that might come its way.

Sometimes Nelson found that a symbol of progress could be as powerful and influential as any new law. In 1995 South Africa hosted the

CONSTITUTION

A constitution is a set of laws that governs an organization or country. The new South African constitution ensured the government was ruled by the majority, in which all people of all colors and religions were eligible to vote. Those opposing the government would no longer be able to be arrested and imprisoned simply for their beliefs.

Nelson meeting the South African national rugby team, Springboks, at the Rugby World Cup in May 1995.

Rugby World Cup. This was a very important step forward for South Africa. Under the rules of apartheid, black people had not been able to play for the national team, the Springboks. Apartheid might now have been abolished, but bad feeling toward the Springboks remained. This was because most people in the team were still white. The Springboks went on to win the cup. Nelson publicly showed his support for

the Springboks and he encouraged all black citizens to follow his example.

Nelson's interest extended far beyond the South African borders. Whether he wanted it or not, Nelson had become a symbol of Africa as a whole. He used that position to further more improvements. In a speech helping to launch the "Kick Polio Out of Africa" campaign (which used a soccer ball as its symbol), he said, "Africa is renowned for its beauty, its rich natural heritage, and huge resources—but equally, the image of its suffering children haunts the conscience of our continent and the world."

"KICK POLIO OUT OF AFRICA"

Polio is a disease that often leads to loss of movement. It continued to affect people in Africa, especially children, long after it had been removed from most other parts of the world. The campaign against polio encouraged the use of vaccination as a way of getting rid of the disease.

President Nelson Mandela chats with Deputy President Thabo Mbeki as he attends his last cabinet meeting, on June 9, 1999.

Nelson Mandela's whole term as president was dominated by moving on from the oppressive regime of the past, which had kept black people down for so long. Now having reached his eighties, Nelson recognized that it was time to step back from daily political responsibilities. He had long maintained that he would serve only one term—and as so many people already knew about Nelson, he was a man of his word.

Chapter 11

Shifting gears

When Nelson retired from political life in 2004, he was certainly not expecting to disappear from sight.

He had become much more than a high-ranking government figure in South Africa. Nelson was now an international celebrity, and he hoped to use his fame and influence to further worthy causes. Among the organizations he helped to establish was the Nelson Mandela Foundation. Its mission was to help make a just and free society that treated people with fairness, wherever they came from.

Nelson Mandela and singer and activist Bob Geldof speaking at the launch of the Make Poverty History campaign rally in London, England, in 2005.

MAKE POVERTY HISTORY

There was still much Nelson hoped to achieve. He was committed to fighting for human rights around the world. He also fought to raise awareness of the AIDS epidemic. The cumulative effects of AIDS had been devastating. More than 30 million people had been infected around the world. Nelson's son Makhatho died of AIDS in 2005, at the age of 55. Nelson described AIDS as "one of the greatest threats humankind has faced."

WHAT IS AIDS?

AIDS is an infection that attacks the human body's immune system (which helps the body keep free from infection). It is caused by the virus HIV. From the 1980s, AIDS had spread rapidly all over the world. Its effects had been particularly deadly in Africa. Nelson dedicated himself to promoting the cause of making lifesaving drugs more widely available.

Nelson Mandela with AIDS activist Zackie Achmat

Nelson celebrated his 90th birthday surrounded by his grandchildren on July 18, 2008.

Nelson also wanted to spend more time with his family. He could not replace the time he had lost with his children and grandchildren because of prison and his career, but he could at least see them more often now that the daily responsibilities of political life had been removed.

His personal life had also taken another turn. After his divorce from Winnie, he had come to know Graça Machel, a former

education minister in Mozambique. Her husband, Samora Machel, the president of Mozambique, had died in a plane crash in 1986.

Graça was 27 years younger than Nelson, and at first they simply became good friends. While Graça continued her humanitarian work on behalf of refugees, her friendship with Nelson deepened as they spent more and more time together. They were finally married in 1998, just before Mandela's term as president ended.

GRAÇA MACHEL

Graça Machel was born in 1945 and grew up in the southern African country of Mozambique. She attended the University of Lisbon in Portugal, where she first took an interest in issues of independence. When Mozambique declared its independence from Portugal in 1975, she became its first Minister for Education and Culture.

Queen Sofía of Spain talks with Nelson Mandela at a pre-wedding royal dinner in Madrid in 2004.

Nelson Mandela sits with US president George W. Bush in the White House's Oval Office in May 2005.

British prime minister Gordon Brown greets Nelson Mandela at Downing Street, London, in August 2007.

Although he lacked the energy of earlier years, Nelson still traveled widely and hosted leaders who came to visit him. When speaking at the birthday celebration of his friend Walter Sisulu in 2002, he said, "What counts in life is not the mere fact that we have lived."

Nelson continued to face a number of health issues. He had survived several bouts with cancer by the time he decided to formally retire from public life in 2004. He then returned to his home in the village of Qunu where he had lived as a boy so many years before.

"It is **what difference we have made** to the lives of others that will determine **the significance of** the life we lead."

From a speech by Nelson during the 90th birthday celebrations of his friend Walter Sisulu in 2002

But he was not done yet. On his birthday, on July 18, in 2007, Nelson and Graça announced the creation of a new organization, the Elders. Its members were retired political and religious leaders, who viewed themselves as independent world leaders working together for peace and human rights. Membership of the Elders included Kofi Annan, former United Nations Secretary General; Jimmy Carter, former United States President; and Li Zhaoxing, former Foreign Minister of the People's Republic of China. The group's small size reflected Nelson's preference for one-on-one meetings over large organized gatherings. In the years since, they have worked to promote women's equality and dealt with humanitarian crises such as famine.

Nelson's reputation as a worldwide champion of democracy and social justice was further underscored in 2009. On his birthday that year, the United Nations declared July 18 to be forever known as Nelson Mandela International Day in honor of his contributions to peace and human rights. In keeping with Nelson's spirit, the day was not meant to be a holiday, but a day devoted to the idea of making the world a better place for everyone who lives in it.

A year later, in 2010, Nelson made his final public appearance at the end of the soccer World Cup tournament in South Africa. Three years after that, at the age of 95 on December 5, 2013, Nelson died.

South African fans show their support for Nelson at the opening ceremony ahead of the 2010 FIFA World Cup in South Africa.

Nelson and his wife, Graça, wave to the crowd before the 2010 World Cup final between the Netherlands and Spain on July 11.

12

Remembered

Nelson's death itself was not a surprise to his family. They had gathered at his bedside knowing the end was near.

Nelson Mandela had lived through the end of World War I, the entirety of World War II, the invention of frozen foods, television, and cell phones. Explorers in his youth were still circling the globe in ships—now astronauts orbited the Earth from space.

Perhaps most of all, Nelson had witnessed the peaceful growth of incredible political and social change in South Africa. The country was hardly perfect. It had some of the same shortcomings as other countries, such as the inequality between rich and poor. But South Africa had fundamentally transformed from the rigid, racially based society of the early 1900s,

and Nelson had led the charge for that change for more than 70 years.

Jacob Zuma

Upon the news of Nelson's death, Jacob Zuma, the president of South Africa, released a statement. He declared that whether in South Africa or somewhere else in the world, people should continue to follow Nelson's vision of a way of life in which everyone treated one another with respect and fairness. "Let us reaffirm his vision of a society in which none is exploited, oppressed, or dispossessed by another."

CHANGES IN SOUTH AFRICA

By the time of Nelson's death, South Africa was a vibrant part of the international community. This was only possible because of the changes that had come to South Africa. Black people now had the same political rights as white people, which had enormous social, economic, and cultural consequences.

"When a man has done what he considers to be his duty to his country and his people, he can rest in peace."

Nelson Mandela, speaking after suffering from an infection in his nineties

Tributes quickly poured in from all over the world. "Nelson Mandela's shining example and his political legacy of non-violence and the condemnation of all forms of racism will continue to inspire people around the world for many years to come," said German chancellor Angela Merkel. Israeli prime minister Benjamin Netanyahu noted, "He was the father of his people, a man of vision, a freedom fighter who rejected violence." American television talk show host Oprah Winfrey remembered, "Being in his presence was like sitting with grace and majesty at the same time."

Today in South Africa, Nelson Mandela is often called the "Father of the Nation." Throughout his life he was certainly happy to accept a compliment, but he would have been the first to declare that he was far from perfect. He made mistakes like everyone else—but to the world, perhaps his flaws had faded into the background while his better qualities had stepped to the front.

A sea of flowers lies at the road's edge as crowds gather to pay their respects at Nelson Mandela's Johannesburg home. This was only a few days after the former leader's death was announced. Although Mandela had been ill for some time, his death still sparked an outpouring of grief and dismay.

The British leader Winston Churchill, upon hearing one of his opponents described as a modest man, immediately replied that the man had a lot to be modest about. Nelson's supporters and opponents alike described him as a stubborn man. However, considering the oppression and difficulties he had confronted in his lifetime, truly he had much to be stubborn about, too.

Certainly, Nelson could never have survived so many obstacles without a fierce stubbornness to help him through the hard times. His long life had been marked with hurdles: The early death of his father, his interrupted education, his time as a hunted activist, and,

The largest statue of Nelson Mandela in the world is 26 ft (8 m) high. It stands on Naval Hill in Bloemfontein, the city of roses, in South Africa.

most of all, his 27 years in prison, would have broken a lesser man.

Yet this same stubbornness, fed by his faith in the righteousness of his ideals, had not led to anger or resentment. No one would have faulted Nelson for seeking revenge against those who had unjustly harmed him. But Nelson stubbornly resisted taking that path as well. Given what he had endured, he was also the most forgiving of men.

DID YOU KNOW?

Nelson was often called "Madiba" by close friends and family. It was a tribal name bestowed as a sign of great respect.

MADIBA SHIRT

The Madiba shirt, made popular by Nelson, is made of silk and usually has a bold and colorful print. The shirt was named after Nelson's nickname. He wore them often, to social gatherings and more formal business or political meetings. People still wear the Madiba shirt today.

He wrote, "No one is born hating another person because of the colour of his skin, or his background, or his religion. People must learn to hate, and if they can learn to hate, they can be taught to love, for love comes more naturally to the human heart than its opposite."

Nelson Mandela believed that people, whatever their faults, are capable of doing better. Nelson, and the people that he guided, brought freedom and fairness to South Africa and set an example for peace that has inspired others all over the world.

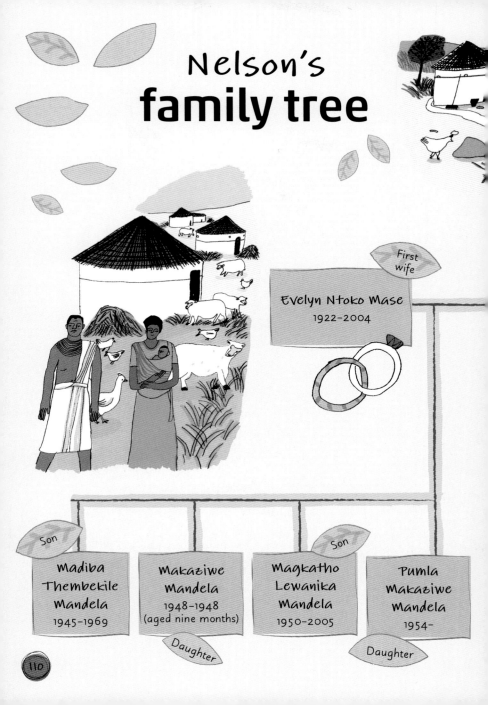

Nelson's family tree

First wife

Evelyn Ntoko Mase
1922–2004

Son

Madiba Thembekile Mandela
1945–1969

Makaziwe Mandela
1948–1948
(aged nine months)

Daughter

Son

Magkatho Lewanika Mandela
1950–2005

Pumla Makaziwe Mandela
1954–

Daughter

110

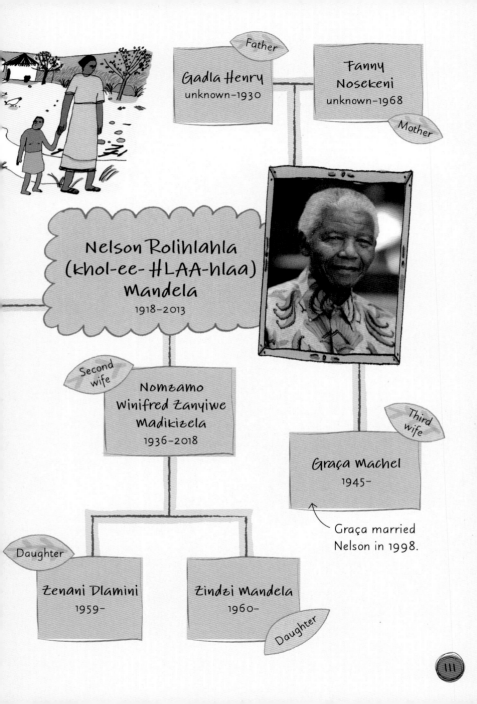

Father

Gadla Henry
unknown–1930

Fanny
Nosekeni
unknown–1968

Mother

Nelson Rolihlahla
(khol-ee-HLAA-hlaa)
Mandela
1918–2013

Second
wife

Nomzamo
Winifred Zanyiwe
Madikizela
1936–2018

Third
wife

Graça Machel
1945–

Graça married
Nelson in 1998.

Daughter

Zenani Dlamini
1959–

Zindzi Mandela
1960–

Daughter

Timeline

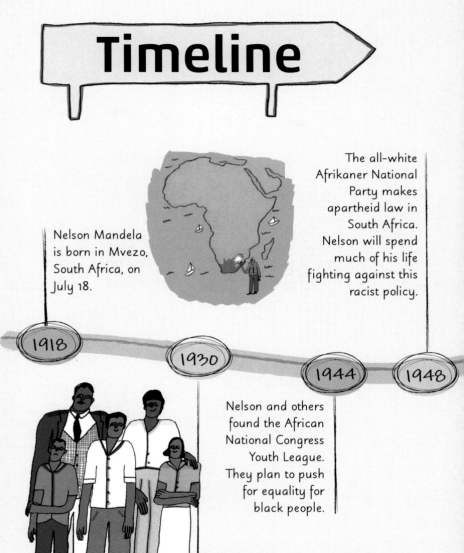

The all-white Afrikaner National Party makes apartheid law in South Africa. Nelson will spend much of his life fighting against this racist policy.

Nelson Mandela is born in Mvezo, South Africa, on July 18.

1918

1930

1944

1948

Nelson and others found the African National Congress Youth League. They plan to push for equality for black people.

Nelson goes to live with Chief Jongintaba Dalindyebo at the Great Place, in Mqhekezweni (mu-KEH-zuh-when-ee).

Nelson marries Winnie
Madikizela on June 14.

Nelson is one
of the leaders of
the ANC's Campaign
for the Defiance
of Unjust Laws.

On March 21, in the
township of Sharpeville,
police open fire on a
crowd of unarmed
protesters, killing 69
people. It became
known as the
Sharpeville Massacre.

1952   1958   1960   1962

Nelson starts a law firm
with his school friend, Oliver
Tambo, to give free or low-cost
legal services to black people
in need.

Nelson is arrested
and accused of
crimes against
the state. He is
sentenced to five
years in prison.

Nelson is tried for more crimes against the government. He is sentenced to life imprisonment and is sent to Robben Island.

Nelson turns 70 in prison. A concert in the UK celebrates his birthday, and 200 million people around the world tune in to watch it on television.

1963–1964

1976

1988

1990

On June 16, police shoot at an unarmed crowd of children marching in protest in the township of Soweto. Twenty-three people die.

After 27 years, Nelson is released from prison.

114

Nelson, jointly with South African president F. W. de Klerk, is awarded the Nobel Peace Prize.

New, free elections are held in South Africa. The ANC wins, and Nelson is elected president.

On July 18, the United Nations declares Nelson's birthday to be Nelson Mandela International Day in honor of his contributions to peace and human rights.

1993   **1994**   **2004**   **2009**   **2013**

After many health issues, Nelson formally retires from public life.

Nelson's autobiography, *Long Walk to Freedom*, is published.

On December 5, at 95 years old, Nelson dies.

Quiz

 In what year did Dutch colonizers come to South Africa?

 When Nelson borrowed his father's pants to wear to school, what did he use for a belt to hold them up?

 What is the name of Nelson's tribe?

 Who was the first white man Nelson shook hands with?

 What political group did Nelson join in Johannesburg?

 Were white people a majority or a minority in South Africa?

 What did Nelson's second wife, Winnie, do for a living when he met her?

Do you remember what you've read? How many of these questions about Nelson's life can you answer?

 What is the name of the prison where Nelson served most of his sentence?

 How many years did Nelson spend in prison?

 How old was Nelson when he took office as president of South Africa?

 At what event did Nelson make his last public appearance?

 What name did Nelson's close friends and family call him?

Answers on page 128

Who's who?

Achmat, Zackie
(1962–) South African
AIDS and gay rights activist

Annan, Kofi
(1938–2018) United Nations
secretary-general from 1997
to 2006

Biko, Steve
(1946–1977) Black People's
Convention leader

Botha, P. W.
(1916–2006) prime minister
(1978–1984) and then
president (1984–1989) of
South Africa

Brown, Gordon
(1951–) British prime
minister from 2007 to 2010

Bush, George H. W.
(1924–2018) president of
the United States from 1989
to 1993

Bush, George W.
(1946–) president of the
United States from 2001
to 2009

Castro, Fidel
(1926–2016) Cuban
revolutionary and president
of Cuba until 2008

Dalindyebo, Jongintaba
(1865–1923) chief who
became Nelson's guardian
after his father's death

de Klerk, F. W.
(1936–) president of
South Africa (1989–1994)

Geldof, Bob
(1951–) Irish singer and
political activist

Harris, Reverend Mr.
(unknown) headmaster of
Clarkebury Boarding
Institute

John Paul II
(1920–2005) Pope and head
of the Catholic Church
from 1978 to 2005

**Joyi, Zwelibhangile
(swoh-lib-haan-geel)**
(unknown) chief who visited
the Great Place

Machel, Graça
(1945–) first education minister in free Mozambique, and Nelson's third wife

Mandela, Gadla Henry
(unknown–1930) Nelson's father

Mandela, Nomzamo Winnie Madikizela
(1936–2018) social worker, political activist, and Nelson's second wife

Mandela, Nosekeni Fanny
(unknown–1968) Nelson's mother

Mbeki, Thabo
(1942–) president of South Africa from 1999 to 2008

Mdingane, Miss
(unknown) Nelson's first teacher

Meligqili (mel-leek-qwee-lee)
(unknown) chief who spoke at Nelson's manhood ceremony

Mitterrand, François
(1916–1996) president of France from 1981 to 1995

Nelson, Admiral Lord
(1758–1805) British naval hero

Ntoko Mase, Evelyn
(1922–2004) Nelson's first wife

Sisulu, Walter
(1912–2003) Nelson's friend in the African National Congress, cousin of his first wife

Sofía, Queen
(1938–) queen of Spain

Tambo, Oliver
(1917–1993) Nelson's school friend with whom he started a law firm in 1952

Thatcher, Margaret
(1925–2013) British prime minister from 1979 to 1990

Zuma, Jacob
(1942–) president of South Africa from 2009 to 2018

Glossary

administer
put something into effect, like a law

advised
gave advice to someone

AIDS
infection that attacks the human immune system, which helps keep the body free from infection

ant-heap
hard dirt above an ant colony

apartheid
formal political, social, and economic separation on the basis of race

arranged marriage
parents or guardians pick marriage partners for their children

benefit
something helpful for a person

chasm
deep hole in the earth

chauffeur
professional driver

colonizer
person who creates and controls a new settlement in a foreign land

colony
settlement controlled by a more powerful country

condemnation
strong statement saying that someone or something is wrong

conscience
feeling that you yourself should do the right thing

constitution
set of laws that governs an organization or country

discipline
using self-control to improve your own behavior

disenchanted
no longer in favor of
something

dispossessed
people who have had land
or belongings taken away
from them

domination
complete control over
someone or something

elite
people of a high class

emancipation
freedom

exile
barred from a country

exploited
person or group used unfairly
by another person or group
for their own advantage

facilities
places built for specific uses

feint
motion used to make an
opponent think you are
attacking one way before
you attack a different way

guardian
person who is responsible
for a child

HIV
virus that causes AIDS

inferior
not as good as something
or someone

ingrained
hard to change

injustice
unfair act that goes against
someone's rights

instituting
putting into practice or
making into law

insubordination
disobeying an order from
a higher authority

kraal
small farm, with just a
few animals and crops,
that supports a
single family

leprosy
disease in which the body wastes away

logic
organized and reasoned method of thinking about something

magistrate
government official who administers certain laws in a specific area

mythical
imaginary, or from a made-up story

oppress
keep down a certain group of people or a person

parry
defend against a blow by pushing it to the side

peasant
poor farm worker

plowboy
boy who leads a plow

polio
disease that often leads to loss of movement

political activism
trying to change things in the government

political prisoner
someone in jail because of their political beliefs

prejudice
unfair feeling against certain people or a person

prohibitions
rules that stop people from doing certain things

red tape
lots of unnecessary paperwork demanded by governments or big business

ruthless
without pity, cruel

sabotage
destroy or damage a plan or property

self-sufficient
able to survive on your own

shepherd
person who cares for sheep

significant
important

slingshot
weapon for shooting small stones, made of a V-shaped stick with a handle, and a rubber band

sophisticate
person who knows a lot about world art, culture, and literature

status
social or political position that a person has compared with others

stern
serious in a severe way

strategy
plan

superior
better than something

thatched
made of dried plant material

townships
neighborhoods in South Africa that were racially segregated during apartheid; only black people lived in townships

transition
change from one state to another

treason
trying to overthrow your country's government

twine
type of string made of two or more strings twisted together

undesirable
person who is not wanted

Index

124

Acknowledgments

DK would like to thank Rebekah Wallin for proofreading; Hilary Bird for the index; and Seeta Parmar for additional editorial work.

The publisher would like to thank the following for their kind permission to reproduce their photographs:
(Key: a-above; b-below/bottom; c-center; f-far; l-left; r-right; t-top)

9 Alamy Stock Photo: Gallo Images (tr). 11 Alamy Stock Photo: De Luan (c). 21 Getty Images: Matthew Willman / Gallo Images (b). 22 Unity Archives - Moravian Archives Herrnhut. 30 Alamy Stock Photo: GL Archive (bl). 31 iStockphoto.com: Hipokrat (tr). 36 Getty Images: Popperfoto (b). 41 akg-images: Africa Media Online (t). 42 Getty Images: Universal History Archive / UIG (bl). 43 Alamy Stock Photo: Archive PL (c). 45 Getty Images: Hulton-Deutsch Collection / Corbis (c). 48 Rex by Shutterstock: Sipa. 49 Alamy Stock Photo: Peter Jordan (br). 53 akg-images: Africa Media Online (br). 55 Rex by Shutterstock: Sipa. 57 Alamy Stock Photo: Blaine Harrington III (t). 61 Alamy Stock Photo: Robertharding. 63 Getty Images: Dave Hogan (t). 66–67 Getty Images: Bongani Mnguni / City Press / Gallo Images (b). 68 Rex by Shutterstock: (bl). 70 Alamy Stock Photo: Peter Jordan (bl). 72 Getty Images: Trevor Samson / AFP (bl). 74–75 Getty Images: David Turnley / Corbis / VCG. 77 Getty Images: Bernard Bisson / Sygma (tr). 83 Getty Images: Walter Dhladhla / AFP (t); Hanner Frankenfeld / AFP (b). 87 Getty Images: Gary Benard / AFP (t). 89 Getty Images: Odd Andersen / AFP (t). 90 Getty Images: Photofusion / UIG (b). 91 Getty Images: Anna Zieminski / AFP (br).

92 Getty Images: Themba Hadebe / AFP (t). 93 Getty Images: Per-Anders Pettersson (br). 94 Getty Images: Alberto Martin / AFP (tc); Mannie Garcia (cr); Cate Gillon (bc). 99 Getty Images: Pierre-Philippe Marcou / AFP (b); Cameron Spencer (t). 101 Getty Images: Unkel / ullstein bild (tr). 104–105 Getty Images: Erhan Sevenler / Anadolu Agency. 106 Dreamstime.com: Grobler Du Preez. 109 Getty Images: Louise Gubb / Corbis SABA. 111 Getty Images: Chris Jackson (cr)

Cover images: *Front:* Alamy Stock Photo: Interfoto b; *Spine:* Alamy Stock Photo: Interfoto ca

All other images © Dorling Kindersley
For further information see: www.dkimages.com

ANSWERS TO THE QUIZ ON PAGES 116–117

1. 1652; 2. A rope; 3. The Xhosa; 4. Reverend Mr. Harris, Clarkebury Boarding Institute Headmaster; 5. The African National Congress (ANC); 6. A minority (always have been); 7. She was a social worker; 8. Robben Island; 9. 27; 10. 77; 11. The soccer World Cup finals in South Africa in 2010; 12. Madiba

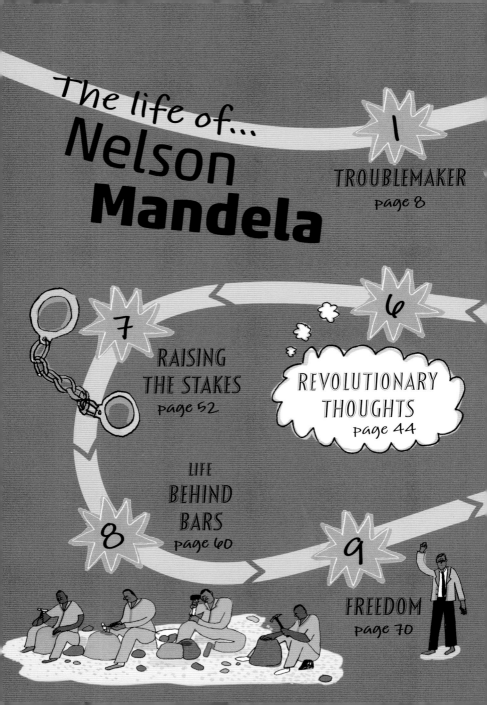

The life of...
Nelson Mandela

Dear Reader,

Nelson Mandela was a man of his time. How could he not be? There was no way for him to ignore the challenging circumstances of his childhood and young adult years. Born into a deeply prejudiced South Africa in 1918, he grew up to witness firsthand his country's official apartheid policy.

And yet he was a man whose actions transcended his own time as well. His enemies released him in 1990 after 27 years of imprisonment. At such a moment, many leaders in his position would have sought revenge under the guise of justice.

But not Nelson. What did he do instead? He showed a remarkable capacity for forgiveness, a willingness to put the past aside and concentrate on the future. As he stated so clearly, "If you want to make peace with your enemy, then you have to work with your enemy. Then he becomes your partner."

Nelson Mandela bravely partnered with the white South Africans that had kept the black population under their thumbs for so long. In doing so, he both saved his country and set an example to the world.

Stephen Krensky

Penguin
Random
House

Senior Editors Marie Greenwood, Allison Singer, Roohi Sehgal
Senior Designer Joanne Clark

Editor Kritika Gupta
Art Editor Kanika Kalra
Jacket Coordinator Issy Walsh
Jacket Designer Dheeraj Arora
DTP Designers Sachin Gupta, Ashok Kumar
Picture Researcher Aditya Katyal
Pre-Producer Sophie Chatellier
Producer Amy Knight
Managing Editors Laura Gilbert, Monica Saigal
Deputy Managing Art Editor Ivy Sengupta
Managing Art Editor Diane Peyton Jones
Delhi Team Head Malavika Talukder
Creative Director Helen Senior
Publishing Director Sarah Larter

Subject Consultant Dr. Matthew Graham
Literacy Consultant Stephanie Laird

First American Edition, 2019
Published in the United States by DK Publishing
1450 Broadway, Suite 801, New York, NY 10018
Copyright © 2019 Dorling Kindersley Limited

DK, a Division of Penguin Random House LLC
19 20 21 22 23 10 9 8 7 6 5 4 3 2 1
001–314132–July/2019

A catalog record for this book is available from the Library of Congress.
ISBN: 978-1-4654-8400-0 (Paperback)
ISBN: 978-1-4654-8399-7 (Hardcover)

DK books are available at special discounts when purchased in bulk for sales promotions,
premiums, fund-raising, or educational use. For details, contact:
DK Publishing Special Markets, 1450 Broadway, Suite 801, New York, NY 10018
SpecialSales@dk.com

Printed and bound in China

A WORLD OF IDEAS:
SEE ALL THERE IS TO KNOW

www.dk.com

DK Life Stories

Nelson
MANDELA

by Stephen Krensky

Illustrated by Charlotte Ager